STOP BEING FAKE

A GUIDE TO OVERCOMING PRETENSE AND EMBRACING GENUINE LIVING FOR A FULFILLING LIFE

By

PRINCE WILLIAM

Copyright @ 2024 Prince William
All rights reserved.

Table of Contents

INTRODUCTION

Prince William delivers a groundbreaking guide to reclaiming authenticity in "Stop Being Fake." Drawing from his own experiences navigating public scrutiny and societal pressures, Prince William offers a compelling roadmap for individuals yearning to break free from the shackles of pretense and live genuinely.

"Stop Being Fake" is more than just a self-help book; it's a call to arms against the pervasive culture of superficiality. Through poignant anecdotes and practical advice, Prince William empowers readers to shed the layers of deceit and embrace their true selves unapologetically.

With unwavering honesty, Prince William dissects the root causes of inauthenticity, offering profound insights into the detrimental effects of living a counterfeit life. From societal expectations to fear of judgment, he addresses the myriad factors that contribute to the fabrication of identity, urging readers to confront these barriers head-on.

This transformative guide doesn't merely highlight the problem—it provides actionable strategies for change. Prince William shares invaluable techniques for cultivating self-awareness, fostering genuine connections, and aligning actions with values. With each chapter, readers are encouraged to embark on a journey of self-discovery and rediscover the liberating power of authenticity.

"Stop Being Fake" is a beacon of hope for anyone trapped in the cycle of pretense. Through Prince William's compassionate guidance, readers will gain the courage to dismantle their masks, embrace vulnerability, and live authentically. It's time to stop pretending and start living—because in the pursuit of authenticity, there is nothing to lose, and everything to gain.

CHAPTER ONE

RECOGNIZING AUTHENTICITY

Recognizing authenticity in behavior involves the ability to discern when individuals are acting in alignment with their true selves, rather than conforming to external expectations or societal norms. Authentic behavior is characterized by honesty, transparency, congruence between actions and values, and a genuine expression of one's thoughts and emotions.

By cultivating the skill of recognizing authenticity, individuals can foster their journey toward self-actualization. This process, as described by psychologist Abraham Maslow, involves realizing one's full potential and striving for personal growth and fulfillment.

When individuals authentically express themselves, they are more likely to make choices that resonate with their inner values and aspirations. This authenticity fosters a sense of congruence between their internal experiences and external behaviors, leading to increased self-awareness and a deeper understanding of their own needs and desires.

Furthermore, authenticity promotes genuine connections with others, as people are drawn to those who are sincere and true to themselves. These meaningful connections provide opportunities for support, feedback, and validation, which are essential components of personal growth and self-actualization.

As individuals become more attuned to authentic behavior, they become empowered to make choices that reflect their true selves, leading to greater fulfillment and satisfaction in life. This journey toward self-actualization is characterized by a sense of authenticity, purpose, and inner peace, as individuals live in alignment with their deepest values and aspirations.

UNDERSTANDING AUTHENTICITY

Understanding authenticity involves being true to oneself, expressing one's thoughts, feelings, and beliefs genuinely, without pretense or conformity to societal expectations. It entails aligning actions with inner values and convictions, fostering a sense of congruence between one's inner and outer selves. Authenticity encompasses self-awareness, self-acceptance, and the courage to embrace vulnerability. Reasons why many people struggle to be authentic stem from various societal, cultural, and psychological factors. Society often imposes rigid norms and standards, leading individuals to prioritize conformity over authenticity to gain acceptance or avoid judgment. Fear of rejection or criticism inhibits authentic expression, fostering a facade to fit in or meet external expectations. Moreover, past experiences of invalidation or trauma can hinder the development of a strong sense of self, making it challenging to authentically engage with others.

Understanding authenticity involves introspection, acknowledging one's values, desires, and emotions, and accepting them without judgment. It requires cultivating self-compassion and embracing imperfections as integral parts of the human experience. Recognizing authenticity in behavior involves discerning genuine expressions from superficial or manipulative ones. Authentic behavior emanates sincerity, transparency, and a genuine connection with oneself and others, fostering trust and intimacy in relationships.

Authenticity is a cornerstone of self-actualization, the process of realizing one's full potential and achieving personal fulfillment. By embracing authenticity, individuals cultivate a deeper sense of self-awareness and autonomy, allowing them to make choices aligned with their values and aspirations. Authenticity fosters genuine connections with others, fostering meaningful relationships based on mutual understanding and acceptance. It empowers individuals to navigate life's challenges with resilience and integrity, fostering growth and self-discovery.

Self-actualization entails living authentically, pursuing goals and passions that resonate with one's authentic self. It involves transcending societal expectations and embracing individuality, fostering a sense of purpose and fulfillment. Authenticity liberates individuals from the constraints of social conditioning, allowing them to live life on their terms, unapologetically and with integrity. By honoring their true selves, individuals unlock their innate potential, leading to a more meaningful and fulfilling existence.

Summarily, understanding authenticity involves being true to oneself, while recognizing authenticity in behavior entails discerning genuine expressions from superficial ones. Authenticity is essential for self-actualization, empowering individuals to live authentically, pursue their passions, and cultivate meaningful connections with others. Despite societal pressures and personal insecurities, embracing authenticity is key to unlocking one's true potential and leading a fulfilling life.

IDENTIFYING FAKE BEHAVIORS

Fake behaviors refer to actions, expressions, or attitudes that are insincere or deceptive, often motivated by a desire to manipulate others' perceptions or outcomes. These behaviors can manifest in various contexts, such as social interactions, relationships, or professional settings. Identifying fake behaviors requires attentiveness to inconsistencies, lack of authenticity, and underlying motives.

Detecting fake behaviors in oneself can be a challenging but crucial endeavor for personal growth and genuine connection with others. One common example of fake behavior is exemplified by someone who constantly seeks validation from others by exaggerating achievements or fabricating stories to impress. Let's delve deeper into this scenario to understand the character traits and underlying reasons behind such behavior.

Consider Sarah, a young professional striving to make a mark in her industry. Sarah exhibits several fake behaviors rooted in insecurity and the desire for external validation. One of Sarah's traits is excessive self-promotion. In meetings or social gatherings, she often dominates conversations with grandiose tales of her accomplishments, embellishing details to garner admiration. This behavior stems from Sarah's deep-seated insecurity about her abilities and fear of being perceived as inadequate.

Furthermore, Sarah demonstrates insincerity in her interactions. She feigns interest in others' achievements but quickly redirects the conversation back to herself. Her compliments feel forced and lack genuine warmth, serving as a means to elicit praise in return. This lack of authenticity erodes trust and undermines genuine connections with colleagues and peers.

Another characteristic of Sarah's fake behavior is her tendency to deflect criticism or feedback. When confronted with constructive criticism, she becomes defensive and dismissive, refusing to acknowledge areas for improvement. This defensive posture shields Sarah from confronting her insecurities and facing the possibility of failure. Instead of embracing feedback as an opportunity for growth, she perceives it as a threat to her carefully crafted facade of success.

Behind these traits lie deeper psychological motives driving Sarah's fake behavior. Her constant need for validation stems from a fear of rejection and a fragile sense of self-worth. By seeking external approval, Sarah attempts to validate her worthiness and quell her inner doubts. However, this cycle of validation-seeking only perpetuates feelings of emptiness and inadequacy, as genuine self-esteem cannot be derived solely from external sources.

Moreover, Sarah's reluctance to acknowledge her shortcomings reflects a fear of vulnerability and a rigid adherence to perfectionism. Admitting imperfections would shatter the illusion of flawlessness she meticulously maintains. Thus, Sarah resorts to defensive mechanisms to preserve her self-image, even at the expense of personal growth and authentic relationships.

So identifying and addressing fake behaviors requires introspection, self-awareness, and a willingness to confront uncomfortable truths. In the case of Sarah, her fake behaviors stem from deep-seated insecurities, fear of rejection, and a relentless pursuit of external validation. By acknowledging these underlying motives and cultivating genuine self-esteem, individuals can transcend fake behaviors and cultivate authentic connections built on honesty and vulnerability.

PRACTICE

Practical Task 1: Reflective Journaling

Task Description: Set aside time each day for reflective journaling. Use this time to explore your thoughts, feelings, and experiences related to authenticity. Reflect on moments when you felt most genuine and aligned with your true self, as well as instances when you may have veered away from authenticity due to external pressures or fears. Consider the values, beliefs, and passions that resonate deeply with you and how you can incorporate them more fully into your daily life. Challenge yourself to identify any patterns or barriers that may be hindering your authenticity and brainstorm strategies for overcoming them. Be honest and open with yourself as you engage in this self-exploration process.

Task Objective: Reflective journaling encourages self-awareness and introspection, helping you to recognize and acknowledge your authentic self. By examining your thoughts and behaviors, you can gain deeper insights into what authenticity means to you and how you can cultivate it in your life.

Practical Task 2: Authenticity Audit

Task Description: Conduct an authenticity audit of your daily interactions and activities. Pay close attention to moments when you may be presenting a facade or conforming to societal expectations rather than expressing your true self. Take note of any discrepancies between how you present yourself to others and how you genuinely feel inside. Identify areas of your life where you feel most authentic and areas where you may need to make adjustments to align with your true values and beliefs. Consider seeking feedback from trusted friends or family members to gain additional perspective on your authenticity.

Task Objective: The authenticity audit provides an opportunity to evaluate your current level of authenticity and identify areas for growth. By shining a light on areas where you may be living inauthentically, you can take proactive steps to realign your actions and behaviors with your authentic self.

Practical Task 3: Authenticity Challenges

Task Description: Engage in authenticity challenges designed to push you outside of your comfort zone and encourage genuine self-expression. These challenges could include tasks such as speaking up about your true feelings or opinions in a group setting, setting boundaries with others to prioritize your own needs, or pursuing a passion or interest that you've been hesitant to explore. Start with small, manageable challenges and gradually increase the difficulty as you become more comfortable with embracing authenticity.

Task Objective: Authenticity challenges provide opportunities for practical application of authentic living principles. By stepping outside of your comfort zone and taking risks, you can build confidence in your ability to be true to yourself in various situations. Over time, these challenges can help you cultivate a more authentic and fulfilling life.

CHAPTER TWO

UNVEILING THE MASKS

Unveiling the masks of pretense and fake behaviors is a crucial step towards personal growth and authenticity. It involves peeling away the layers of societal expectations, ingrained habits, and defense mechanisms to reveal your true self. Embracing authenticity fosters genuine connections, self-confidence, and emotional well-being. Here are practical steps and examples to guide you on this transformative journey:

1. **Self-Reflection**: Take time to introspect and identify areas of your life where you may be wearing a mask. Reflect on situations where you feel compelled to act in a certain way to please others or conform to societal norms. Ask yourself why you behave in certain ways and

whether those behaviors align with your true values and beliefs.

Example: *You might realize that you often agree with others even when you have a different opinion to avoid conflict. Reflecting on why you do this can reveal underlying insecurities or a fear of rejection.*

2. Honesty with Yourself: Be brutally honest with yourself about your thoughts, feelings, and motivations. Acknowledge any discomfort or fear that arises when confronting aspects of yourself that you've kept hidden.

Example: *Admitting to yourself that you feel inadequate when you don't meet certain expectations can be uncomfortable but is essential for growth.*

3. Challenge Societal Expectations: Question societal norms and expectations that dictate how you should behave or present yourself. Recognize that conforming to these expectations often involves wearing masks to fit in or gain approval.

Example: *Instead of striving for perfection to meet societal standards, embrace your imperfections and celebrate your unique qualities.*

4. Practice Authentic Communication: Communicate openly and honestly with others, expressing your true thoughts and feelings without fear of judgment or rejection. Authentic communication fosters genuine connections and deepens relationships.

Example: *Instead of pretending to be fine when you're struggling, share your vulnerabilities with a trusted friend or family member. This allows them to offer support and strengthens your bond.*

5. Set Boundaries: Establish boundaries to protect your authentic self from being compromised or manipulated by others. Learn to say no to requests or situations that don't align with your values or well-being.

Example: *If someone consistently disrespects your boundaries, have the courage to confront them and assert your needs.*

6. Seek Support: Surround yourself with people who accept and support you for who you truly are. Build a network of friends, mentors, or therapists who encourage your authenticity and provide guidance on your journey of self-discovery.

Example: *Joining a support group or attending therapy sessions can provide a safe space to explore your authentic self without judgment.*

7. Practice Self-Compassion: Be kind and compassionate towards yourself as you navigate the process of unveiling your masks. Accept that it's okay to be imperfect and that growth takes time and effort.

Example: *Instead of criticizing yourself for past mistakes, offer yourself words of encouragement and forgiveness.*

Unveiling the masks of pretense and fake behaviors is essential for personal growth and transformation. It allows you to live a life aligned with your true values, passions, and aspirations. By embracing authenticity, you cultivate deeper connections with others, enhance your self-confidence, and experience greater fulfillment and joy. So, embark on this journey with courage and curiosity, knowing that the rewards far outweigh the challenges.

EXAMINING SOCIAL MASKS

In human interaction, we often wear masks – not physical ones, but social ones. These masks are the personas we adopt in different contexts, presenting versions of ourselves tailored to fit social expectations, norms, and roles. Delving into the examination of these social masks can offer profound insights into ourselves and others, enriching our relationships and personal growth.

Firstly, understanding social masks allows us to recognize the complexity of human identity. We are multifaceted beings, shaped by a myriad of influences including culture, upbringing, and personal experiences. Our social masks are like layers of a complex tapestry, revealing different facets of our personality in various social settings. By acknowledging these masks, we move beyond simplistic notions of who we are or who others are, fostering a deeper appreciation for the richness and diversity of human nature.

Moreover, examining social masks cultivates empathy and compassion. When we recognize that everyone wears masks to some extent, we become more understanding of the struggles and insecurities underlying these personas. Empathy flourishes as we realize that behind the confident facade may lie feelings of vulnerability, and beneath the stoic exterior may reside fears and uncertainties. This awareness encourages us to interact with greater kindness and sensitivity, fostering genuine connections built on mutual understanding and acceptance.

Furthermore, exploring social masks promotes authenticity and self-awareness. As we peel back the layers of our own masks, we gain insight into our true desires, values, and aspirations. We discern between societal expectations and our genuine selves, empowering us to live more authentically aligned lives. Embracing our authentic selves fosters a sense of inner peace and fulfillment, as we no longer feel the need to conform to external standards or suppress parts of our identity to fit in.

Additionally, examining social masks facilitates deeper, more meaningful relationships. When we engage with others from a place of authenticity and understanding, our connections become more genuine and profound. By transcending superficial interactions, we forge bonds based on mutual trust, respect, and vulnerability. We create spaces where people feel safe to reveal their true selves, fostering intimacy and camaraderie.

Moreover, exploring social masks can be a catalyst for personal growth and transformation. As we confront the fears, insecurities, and limiting beliefs that underpin our masks, we embark on a journey of self-discovery and self-mastery. We confront our inner demons, embrace our strengths and weaknesses, and cultivate a deeper sense of self-compassion and resilience. This inner work enables us to break free from self-imposed limitations, unlocking our full potential and leading to greater fulfillment and success in life.

In point of fact, examining social masks offers a myriad of benefits that enrich our lives and relationships. By acknowledging the complexity of human identity, fostering empathy and compassion, promoting authenticity and self-awareness, nurturing deeper connections, and catalyzing personal growth, we embark on a journey of profound self-discovery and transformation. As we peel back the layers of our masks and embrace our authentic selves, we not only enrich our own lives but also create a ripple effect of positive change in the world around us.

UNCOVERING PERSONAL MASKS

Uncovering personal masks involves the process of exploring and understanding the layers of identity and behavior that individuals present to the world, often in contrast to their true selves. These masks are formed through various life experiences, societal expectations, and internalized beliefs, and they can obscure authentic emotions, desires, and vulnerabilities. Delving into this process requires self-reflection, honesty, and courage.

Here are some techniques and practices to assist in uncovering personal masks:

1. Self-Reflection: Begin by setting aside time for introspection. Reflect on your thoughts, feelings, and behaviors in different situations. Ask yourself probing questions such as:

✧ What aspects of myself do I tend to hide or suppress?

✧ How do I behave differently in various social settings?

✧ Are there patterns in my behavior that seem incongruent with my true feelings?

✧ What fears or insecurities might be driving me to wear certain masks?

2. Journaling: Writing down your thoughts and feelings can be a powerful tool for uncovering personal masks. Keep a journal where you can freely express yourself without judgment. Write about your experiences, doubts, and uncertainties. Pay attention to recurring themes or emotions that emerge in your writing, as they may indicate areas where you're wearing a mask.

3. Mindfulness Practices: Engage in mindfulness techniques such as meditation, deep breathing, or yoga to cultivate present-moment awareness. Mindfulness helps you observe your thoughts and emotions without attachment or judgment. By becoming more attuned to your inner experiences, you can begin to identify when you're wearing a mask and explore the underlying reasons behind it.

4. Seek Feedback: Trusted friends, family members, or mentors can provide valuable insights into your behavior and personality. Ask for honest feedback about how you come across to others and whether they sense any discrepancies between your outward presentation and inner reality. Be open to constructive criticism, as it can help you uncover blind spots and false personas.

5. Therapy or Counseling: Consider seeking professional help from a therapist or counselor who specializes in identity exploration and self-discovery. Therapy provides a safe and supportive environment to delve into deeper layers of your psyche, confront unresolved issues, and challenge ingrained beliefs and behaviors. A trained therapist can offer guidance and techniques tailored to your specific needs.

6. Creative Expression: Engage in creative activities such as art, music, dance, or writing to express your authentic self. Creativity bypasses the rational mind and taps into deeper layers of consciousness, allowing hidden thoughts and emotions to surface. Experiment with different forms of expression to uncover aspects of yourself that may be obscured by masks.

7. Emotional Vulnerability: Practice being vulnerable with yourself and others. Allow yourself to experience and express a wide range of emotions, even if they feel uncomfortable or unfamiliar. Share your fears, insecurities, and struggles with trusted individuals who can offer support and understanding. Embracing vulnerability fosters genuine connections and dismantles the need for protective masks.

8. Challenge Limiting Beliefs: Identify and challenge limiting beliefs that contribute to the formation of personal masks. Question assumptions about who you should be or how you should behave based on societal norms or past experiences. Replace negative self-talk with affirmations that affirm your inherent worth and authenticity.

Uncovering personal masks is a journey of self-discovery and growth that requires patience, curiosity, and self-compassion. By peeling back the layers of identity that have been constructed over time, you can reconnect with your true essence and live more authentically. Remember that it's okay to feel vulnerable and uncertain along the way – embracing your authentic self is a courageous act that leads to greater fulfillment and authenticity in life.

PRACTICE

Task 1: Self-Reflection Journaling

Objective: Encourage individuals to engage in deep self-reflection to uncover and understand the masks they wear in different aspects of their lives.

Instructions:

- ✧ Set aside dedicated time each day for self-reflection journaling.

- ✧ Begin by asking yourself probing questions such as:

- ✧ What roles do I play in my life (e.g., friend, employee, family member)?

- ✧ How do I behave differently in each role?

- ✧ Are there aspects of my identity that I hide or downplay in certain situations?

- ✧ What fears or insecurities might be driving me to wear these masks?

- ✧ Write freely and without judgment, allowing your thoughts and feelings to flow onto the page.

- ✧ Review your journal entries regularly to identify patterns and insights about the masks you wear.

Use this newfound awareness to begin peeling away the layers of pretense and embracing your authentic self in all aspects of your life.

Task 2: Authenticity Challenge

Objective: Encourage individuals to step outside their comfort zones and practice authenticity in everyday interactions.

Instructions:

✧ Identify three situations or interactions in your daily life where you tend to hide behind a mask or suppress your true thoughts and feelings.

✧ For each situation, set a specific goal for practicing authenticity (e.g., expressing your true opinions, setting boundaries, being vulnerable).

✧ Prior to each interaction, take a moment to center yourself and connect with your authentic self.

✧ During the interaction, focus on being genuine and true to yourself, even if it feels uncomfortable or risky.

✧ Reflect on each experience afterward, noting any challenges or breakthroughs you encountered.

Celebrate your courage and progress, and use these experiences as stepping stones towards living a more authentic life.

Task 3: Authenticity Circle

Objective: Create a supportive community where individuals can share their struggles and triumphs on the journey to authenticity.

Instructions:

✧ Form a small group of trusted friends, family members, or colleagues who are committed to authenticity and personal growth.

◇ Schedule regular meetings or gatherings to discuss topics related to authenticity, such as vulnerability, self-acceptance, and overcoming fears.

◇ Create a safe and non-judgmental space where each member can share their experiences, challenges, and insights openly and honestly.

◇ Encourage active listening, empathy, and support among group members, providing encouragement and validation for each other's journeys.

◇ Set collective goals or challenges to practice authenticity together, such as sharing a personal story or confronting a fear.

Hold each other accountable and celebrate successes along the way, recognizing that authenticity is a journey best traveled together.

CHAPTER THREE

EMBRACING VULNERABILITY

Embracing vulnerability is a concept that often runs counter to our instincts. We're wired to protect ourselves, to shield our weaknesses, and present a façade of strength to the world. However, understanding the need to embrace vulnerability is crucial for personal growth, building authentic relationships, and fostering resilience.

Vulnerability is not a weakness; it's a strength. It's the courage to show up and be seen, even when there are no guarantees of success or acceptance. When we allow ourselves to be vulnerable, we open the door to genuine connections with others. Think about it - the moments when we've felt closest to someone are often when we've shared our fears, insecurities, and struggles. It's in those moments of vulnerability that true intimacy is born.

Moreover, embracing vulnerability is essential for personal growth. When we're willing to acknowledge our vulnerabilities, we create space for learning and improvement. It's through facing our fears and limitations that we discover our strengths and capabilities. Growth requires stepping out of our comfort zones, taking risks, and being willing to fail. And that requires vulnerability.

Consider the example of starting a new job or pursuing a passion project. It's natural to feel uncertain and exposed in these situations. But it's precisely by embracing vulnerability that we open ourselves up to new experiences and opportunities for growth. By acknowledging our limitations and seeking help when needed, we can learn and develop in ways we never thought possible.

Furthermore, embracing vulnerability is crucial for building resilience. Life is full of challenges and setbacks, and it's how we respond to them that ultimately defines us. Resilience isn't about avoiding vulnerability; it's about facing it head-on and bouncing back stronger. When we're willing to be vulnerable, we're better equipped to handle adversity with grace and courage.

Think about a time when you faced a major setback or disappointment. Perhaps you experienced a failure at work or went through a difficult breakup. In those moments, it's natural to feel exposed and vulnerable. But it's also an opportunity to cultivate resilience - to pick ourselves up, dust ourselves off, and keep moving forward. And it's often through embracing vulnerability that we find the strength to do so.

Moreover, embracing vulnerability is essential for fostering creativity and innovation. When we're willing to take risks and explore new ideas, we open ourselves up to the possibility of failure - but also to the potential for ground-breaking discoveries and breakthroughs. Some of the most innovative ideas and inventions have come from individuals who were willing to embrace vulnerability and think outside the box.

Finally, embracing vulnerability is crucial for living a life of authenticity and fulfillment. When we're constantly trying to hide our flaws and weaknesses, we end up living a life that's inauthentic and unfulfilling. True fulfillment comes from embracing who we are - flaws and all - and showing up in the world as our genuine selves.

No doubt embracing vulnerability is not easy, but it's essential for personal growth, building authentic relationships, fostering resilience, and living a life of authenticity and fulfillment. It's about having the courage to show up and be seen, even when it's scary or uncomfortable. So, let go of the need to appear invulnerable and embrace the beauty and strength that comes from being vulnerable.

THE POWER OF VULNERABILITY

Perfection is often glorified and overrated, but vulnerability stands out as a beacon of authenticity. It's the raw, unfiltered expression of our true selves, devoid of pretense or facade. While vulnerability may seem daunting, it holds immense power in freeing us from the shackles of fake living.

At its core, vulnerability is the courage to show up as we are, imperfections and all. It's about embracing our flaws, fears, and insecurities instead of hiding them behind a mask of false confidence. When we allow ourselves to be vulnerable, we invite genuine connections with others because vulnerability breeds empathy and understanding.

One of the greatest misconceptions about vulnerability is that it signifies weakness. In reality, it takes immense strength to be vulnerable. It requires us to confront our deepest fears of rejection and judgment and to trust that others will accept us for who we truly are. When we embrace vulnerability, we cultivate resilience and inner fortitude, enabling us to navigate life's challenges with authenticity and grace.

Fake living, on the other hand, is built on a foundation of illusion. It's the pursuit of external validation at the expense of our true selves. Whether we're striving to meet society's expectations, comparing ourselves to others on social media, or suppressing our emotions to avoid appearing weak, fake living disconnects us from our authentic essence.

The antidote to fake living is vulnerability. When we allow ourselves to be vulnerable, we break free from the confines of societal norms and expectations. We no longer feel the need to conform to unrealistic standards or hide behind a facade of perfection. Instead, we embrace our humanity—the messy, imperfect, beautiful truth of who we are.

Moreover, vulnerability fosters genuine connections with others. When we open up about our struggles and insecurities, we create space for intimacy and empathy. Authentic relationships are built on a foundation of vulnerability, where both parties feel seen, heard, and accepted for who they truly are. In a world where superficiality often reigns supreme, genuine connections are a rare and precious commodity.

Furthermore, vulnerability is essential for personal growth and self-discovery. When we allow ourselves to be vulnerable, we confront our limitations and fears head-on. We recognize that vulnerability is not a sign of weakness but rather a catalyst for transformation. By embracing vulnerability, we step into our power and unlock our full potential.

In essence, vulnerability is the key to living a life of authenticity and fulfillment. It empowers us to shed the layers of fake living and embrace our true selves unapologetically. When we embrace vulnerability, we cultivate deeper connections, foster personal growth, and experience a profound sense of freedom.

So, how can we harness the power of vulnerability in our own lives? It starts with self-awareness and self-compassion. We must be willing to acknowledge our fears and insecurities without judgment and treat ourselves with kindness and understanding. From there, we can gradually lean into vulnerability by sharing our authentic selves with others and embracing the discomfort that comes with it.

Surely, vulnerability is not a weakness to be avoided but a strength to be embraced. It is the antidote to fake living, allowing us to break free from the constraints of societal expectations and cultivate a life of authenticity and fulfillment. By embracing vulnerability, we invite deeper connections, foster personal growth, and unleash our true potential. So, let us embrace vulnerability wholeheartedly and embark on the journey toward living our most authentic lives.

OVERCOMING FEAR OF AUTHENTICITY

Overcoming the fear of authenticity is a crucial step towards living a genuine and fulfilling life. Authenticity, defined as being true to oneself and one's values, can indeed be a potent force in eliminating fake living. However, it's understandable that fear may arise when considering the implications of embracing authenticity, especially in a world where conformity and societal expectations often hold sway. To navigate this fear and embrace authenticity, a pragmatic approach can be immensely helpful.

Firstly, it's essential to recognize that fear is a natural response to change and uncertainty. Authenticity often requires stepping outside of one's comfort zone and challenging existing norms. However, by reframing fear as a signal that you're moving in the right direction, it becomes a catalyst for growth rather than a barrier. Embrace the discomfort as a sign of progress towards a more authentic way of living.

Secondly, cultivate self-awareness. Understand your values, passions, strengths, and weaknesses. Take time to reflect on what truly matters to you and what brings you joy and fulfillment. This self-awareness serves as a compass guiding your decisions and actions towards authenticity. Journaling, meditation, or seeking feedback from trusted friends and mentors can aid in this process of self-discovery.

Next, challenge limiting beliefs. Often, fear of authenticity stems from ingrained beliefs about what it means to be accepted or successful. Question these beliefs and consider whether they align with your authentic self. Recognize that authenticity doesn't mean perfection; it means embracing your flaws and imperfections as integral parts of who you are. Understand that authenticity is not about seeking approval from others but about staying true to yourself.

Another pragmatic approach is to take small steps towards authenticity. It's not necessary to overhaul your entire life overnight. Start by making small changes aligned with your values and gradually expand from there. This could involve setting boundaries, speaking up for yourself, pursuing hobbies or interests that genuinely resonate with you, or surrounding yourself with people who support and encourage your authentic self-expression.

Moreover, seek out role models who exemplify authenticity. Seeing others living authentically can provide inspiration and validation for your own journey. It reminds you that authenticity is not only possible but also rewarding. Engage with their stories, learn from their experiences, and draw strength from their courage to be true to themselves.

Additionally, practice self-compassion. Understand that embracing authenticity is a process fraught with challenges and setbacks. Be kind to yourself during moments of doubt or fear. Celebrate your progress, no matter how small, and forgive yourself for any perceived missteps along the way. Remember that authenticity is a journey, not a destination, and each step forward is a victory in itself.

Furthermore, cultivate a supportive environment. Surround yourself with people who appreciate and celebrate your authenticity. Seek out communities or groups where you can connect with like-minded individuals who share your values and aspirations. Having a support network can provide encouragement and validation, making it easier to stay true to yourself in the face of external pressures.

Finally, practice mindfulness and resilience. Stay present in the moment and focus on the here and now rather than worrying about future judgments or outcomes. Develop resilience to overcome obstacles and setbacks, recognizing that each challenge is an opportunity for growth and learning.

REAL LIFE EXAMPLES

Several well-known individuals from various fields have openly embraced vulnerability and authenticity, breaking away from the facade of a "fake" life. Here are a few global examples:

1. Brene Brown: Brene Brown is a research professor at the University of Houston and a bestselling author known for her work on vulnerability, courage, and shame. Through her TED Talks, books like "The Gifts of Imperfection," and her research, Brown has inspired millions to embrace vulnerability as a pathway to living wholeheartedly and authentically.

2. Ellen DeGeneres: Ellen DeGeneres, a prominent comedian, actress, and television host, faced significant backlash when she came out as gay in the late 1990s. Despite the challenges and criticism she encountered, DeGeneres remained true to herself, openly embracing her identity and advocating for LGBTQ+ rights. Her authenticity has made her a beloved figure and a role model for many.

3. Viola Davis: Viola Davis, an award-winning actress known for her roles in films like "Fences" and "The Help," has been vocal about her experiences with poverty, racism, and self-doubt. Through her authenticity and vulnerability, Davis has become a powerful advocate for diversity, inclusion, and representation in Hollywood, inspiring others to embrace their unique stories and backgrounds.

4. Prince Harry: Prince Harry, a member of the British royal family, has spoken candidly about his struggles with mental health issues, including grief and trauma stemming from the death of his mother, Princess Diana. In recent years, Harry has become a vocal advocate for mental health awareness, using his platform to encourage open conversations and reduce stigma surrounding mental illness.

5. Lady Gaga: Lady Gaga, a Grammy-winning singer, songwriter, and actress, has been open about her experiences with mental health challenges, including depression, anxiety, and PTSD. Through her music, public appearances, and advocacy work, Gaga has encouraged others to embrace their vulnerabilities and seek support when needed. She founded the Born This

Way Foundation, which focuses on promoting kindness, mental wellness, and acceptance among young people.

6. Dwayne "The Rock" Johnson: Dwayne Johnson, a former professional wrestler turned actor and producer, has spoken openly about his struggles with depression and adversity throughout his life. Despite facing numerous setbacks and failures, Johnson has remained resilient and authentic, sharing his journey with honesty and humility. His authenticity has endeared him to fans worldwide and inspired many to persevere in the face of challenges.

These individuals exemplify the power of vulnerability and authenticity in overcoming adversity, breaking down barriers, and inspiring positive change. By embracing their true selves and sharing their stories openly, they have not only transformed their own lives but also empowered countless others to do the same.

PRACTICE

Practical Tasks:

1. Journaling Prompts:

Task: Set aside dedicated time each day for reflective journaling.

Instructions: Begin by identifying one vulnerability or fear that you've been avoiding. Write freely about why it makes you feel uncomfortable and the impact it has on your life. Then, challenge yourself to reframe this vulnerability as a source of strength or growth opportunity. Explore how embracing this vulnerability could lead to greater authenticity and connection with others. End each entry with one action step you can take to lean into this vulnerability.

2. Vulnerability Conversations:

Task: Initiate open and honest conversations with trusted friends or family members.

Instructions: Choose someone you feel comfortable with and express your desire to deepen your connection through vulnerability. Share one aspect of yourself that you've been hesitant to reveal due to fear or insecurity. Be transparent about why you've held back and the emotions it evokes. Encourage reciprocal sharing by creating a safe space for the other person to express their vulnerabilities as well. Practice active listening and empathy throughout the conversation, focusing on understanding rather than fixing.

3. Creative Expression:

Task: Engage in a creative activity that allows you to express your vulnerabilities.

Instructions: Select a form of creative expression that resonates with you, such as writing, drawing, painting, or music. Use this medium as a tool to explore and communicate your innermost thoughts and feelings. Let go of self-judgment and perfectionism, allowing your vulnerability to flow freely onto the canvas or page. Embrace the process as a cathartic release and an opportunity for self-discovery. Reflect on the experience afterward, noting any insights gained or emotions processed through your creative expression.

CHAPTER FOUR

CULTIVATING SELF-AWARENESS

In the journey towards authenticity and genuine self-expression, one of the most potent tools at our disposal is self-awareness. Defined as the conscious knowledge of one's own character, feelings, motives, and desires, self-awareness serves as a guiding light illuminating the path towards living a life that is true to oneself. It is the cornerstone upon which authenticity is built, empowering individuals to navigate the complexities of existence with clarity, purpose, and integrity.

Cultivating self-awareness begins with a willingness to embark on an introspective journey, delving into the depths of our psyche to uncover the intricacies of our inner world. It involves peeling back the layers of conditioning, societal expectations, and external influences to reveal the authentic essence that lies beneath. This process requires courage, vulnerability, and a commitment to self-discovery.

At its core, self-awareness is about understanding who we are, what we stand for, and what brings us meaning and fulfillment. It involves examining our values, beliefs, strengths, weaknesses, fears, and desires with honesty and compassion. By shining a light on these aspects of ourselves, we gain clarity about what truly matters to us and what we want to prioritize in our lives.

Moreover, self-awareness enables us to recognize the ways in which our thoughts, emotions, and behaviors shape our experiences and interactions with the world around us. It allows us to observe ourselves with curiosity and non-judgment, acknowledging both our light and shadow aspects without succumbing to self-criticism or denial. In doing so, we cultivate a deeper understanding of our patterns and tendencies, empowering us to make conscious choices that align with our authentic selves.

Self-awareness also fosters empathy and compassion towards ourselves and others. By recognizing our own humanity, with all its complexities and imperfections, we develop greater empathy for the struggles and challenges faced by those around us. This empathy becomes a catalyst for deeper connections and more meaningful relationships, as we learn to relate to others from a place of understanding and acceptance.

Furthermore, self-awareness serves as a compass guiding our decisions and actions in alignment with our values and aspirations. It enables us to discern between fleeting desires and authentic longings, allowing us to pursue paths that resonate with our true selves rather than succumbing to external pressures or societal norms. In this way, self-awareness empowers us to live with integrity and authenticity, honoring our own truth even in the face of adversity or opposition.

As we cultivate self-awareness, we become increasingly attuned to the signals and whispers of our inner wisdom, learning to trust our intuition and follow the guidance of our authentic selves. This inner guidance becomes a source of strength and resilience, guiding us through life's challenges and uncertainties with grace and fortitude.

Summarily, self-awareness is a powerful catalyst for authenticity, empowering us to live with clarity, purpose, and integrity. By cultivating self-awareness, we gain insight into who we are, what we stand for, and what brings us meaning and fulfillment. We develop empathy and compassion towards ourselves and others, fostering deeper connections and more meaningful relationships. And we learn to trust our inner wisdom, allowing it to guide us on the journey towards living a life that is true to ourselves.

EXPLORING SELF-REFLECTION

In the cacophony of our daily lives, amidst the hustle and bustle of responsibilities and expectations, there exists a silent yet powerful practice waiting to be embraced: self-reflection. It's a journey inward, a chance to pause and gaze into the mirror of our souls, to unravel the complexities of our thoughts, emotions, and experiences. In a world often driven by external validation and incessant distractions, self-reflection offers a pragmatic path to understanding ourselves and navigating life's twists and turns.

For many, the concept of self-reflection may conjure images of solitary contemplation or philosophical musings. Yet, in its essence, it is a profoundly human endeavor, accessible to all, regardless of background or belief. It's about taking a moment to check in with ourselves, to assess where we are, where we've been, and where we're headed. It's a practice that invites us to confront our fears, confront our weaknesses, and celebrate our strengths.

But how does one embark on this journey of self-reflection, especially in a world that often prioritizes productivity over introspection? The answer lies in weaving self-reflection into the fabric of our daily lives, making it a natural and integral part of our existence. It's not about setting aside hours of uninterrupted solitude (though that can be beneficial), but rather about finding moments of quietude amidst the noise, moments to pause, breathe, and reflect.

Pragmatism dictates that self-reflection need not be a grandiose affair. It can be as simple as carving out a few minutes each day to sit quietly and observe our thoughts and feelings. It can be jotting down our reflections in a journal before bed or taking a leisurely stroll in nature, allowing the rhythm of our footsteps to sync with the cadence of our thoughts. It can even be engaging in meaningful conversations with loved ones, sharing our innermost thoughts and listening deeply to theirs.

Incorporating self-reflection into our lives doesn't require us to retreat from the world; rather, it empowers us to engage with it more intentionally. By cultivating self-awareness, we become better equipped to navigate life's challenges and seize its opportunities. We gain clarity on our values, aspirations, and priorities, enabling us to make decisions aligned with our authentic selves.

Moreover, self-reflection fosters resilience in the face of adversity. It allows us to confront our failures and setbacks with grace and humility, recognizing them as valuable lessons rather than insurmountable obstacles. It reminds us of our inherent worth and agency, empowering us to chart a course forward with renewed purpose and determination.

But perhaps the most profound aspect of self-reflection is its capacity to cultivate empathy and compassion, both towards ourselves and others. As we delve into the depths of our own humanity, we develop a deeper understanding of the human experience as a whole. We recognize the interconnectedness of all beings, sharing in their joys and sorrows, triumphs and struggles.

In a world plagued by division and discord, this empathy becomes a powerful force for healing and reconciliation. It reminds us that beneath the surface-level differences that often divide us lies a common humanity, a shared longing for connection and belonging. It inspires us to extend kindness and understanding to ourselves and others, fostering a culture of empathy and inclusivity.

In the end, self-reflection is not a luxury reserved for the privileged few but a fundamental aspect of what it means to be human. It's a journey of self-discovery, growth, and transformation, one that unfolds not in grand gestures but in the quiet moments of everyday life. So let us embrace the mirror within, with pragmatism and open hearts, knowing that in seeking to understand ourselves, we ultimately find our place in the world.

HONESTY WITH ONESELF

Honesty with oneself is a virtue both profound and elusive, demanding a journey inward that few are willing to embark upon. Yet, it is this journey that holds the key to unlocking the authenticity of our souls, freeing us from the shackles of self-deception and allowing us to stand unabashedly in the light of our own truth.

Building honesty with oneself is not a task for the faint-hearted; it requires courage, vulnerability, and unwavering commitment. It begins with a willingness to peel back the layers of pretense and facade that we have constructed around ourselves, exposing the raw and unfiltered essence of who we truly are. This journey demands that we confront our deepest fears, insecurities, and vulnerabilities with unflinching honesty, refusing to hide behind the safety of half-truths and illusions.

To build honesty with oneself is to cultivate a sacred space within the chambers of our hearts, where the voice of authenticity reigns supreme. It is a space devoid of judgment or condemnation, where we can confront our flaws and imperfections with compassion and understanding. Here, we must learn to listen to the whispers of our intuition, for it is often in the silence of our innermost thoughts that the truth reveals itself most clearly.

Practicing honesty with oneself is an ongoing journey, requiring diligent self-reflection and introspection. It is a commitment to living with integrity, aligning our thoughts, words, and actions with the deepest truths of our being. It is a willingness to acknowledge when we have strayed from our path, and to course-correct with humility and grace.

At times, practicing honesty with oneself may require us to confront uncomfortable truths that we would rather avoid. It may mean acknowledging our own role in perpetuating patterns of self-sabotage or recognizing when our beliefs and perceptions are clouded by bias or prejudice. Yet, it is in these moments of discomfort that the seeds of growth are sown, for it is only by facing our shadows that we can emerge into the fullness of our light.

To practice honesty with oneself is to embrace vulnerability as a sacred gift, recognizing that it is through our most authentic and unguarded moments that we connect most deeply with ourselves and with others. It is a willingness to embrace the messiness of our humanity, embracing both our strengths and our weaknesses as integral parts of who we are.

In the pursuit of honesty with oneself, there are no shortcuts or quick fixes. It is a journey that unfolds over a lifetime, requiring patience, persistence, and unwavering self-love. It is a journey that invites us to embrace the full spectrum of our emotions, from the depths of despair to the heights of joy, knowing that each experience is a reflection of our truth.

In the end, honesty with oneself is not merely a virtue to be cultivated, but a sacred calling that beckons us to awaken to the fullness of our being. It is a journey of self-discovery and self-reclamation, guiding us back to the essence of who we were always meant to be. And though the path may be fraught with challenges and uncertainties, it is a journey worth embarking upon, for in the depths of our own truth lies the liberation of our souls.

PRACTICE

Practical Tasks:

1. Daily Reflection Practice: Set aside dedicated time each day for introspection and reflection. Journaling can be a powerful tool for this task. Write down your thoughts, feelings, and experiences, and explore questions such as: What are my core values? What brings me joy and fulfillment? What are my strengths and weaknesses? Regular reflection will deepen your self-awareness and help you uncover insights about yourself.

2. Seek Feedback from Trusted Sources: Reach out to friends, family members, mentors, or colleagues whom you trust and respect. Ask them for honest feedback about your strengths, weaknesses, and areas for growth.

Be open to receiving constructive criticism, as it can provide valuable insights into aspects of yourself that you may not have been aware of. Use this feedback to further refine your self-awareness and develop a clearer understanding of your authentic self.

3. Mindful Observation of Reactions: Throughout your day, pay close attention to your reactions and responses in various situations. Notice any patterns or recurring themes in your thoughts, emotions, and behaviors. Ask yourself why you react a certain way in different circumstances and what underlying beliefs or values may be influencing your actions. This practice of mindful observation will deepen your self-awareness and help you gain greater clarity about your authentic identity.

CHAPTER FIVE

BUILDING GENUINE RELATIONSHIPS

Once upon a time, in a bustling city, there lived a young woman named Sarah. Sarah was ambitious and driven, with a passion for her career in marketing. However, amidst the demands of her job and the fast-paced city life, she often found herself feeling disconnected and lonely. Despite having many acquaintances and colleagues, Sarah longed for deeper, more meaningful connections in her life.

One day, Sarah attended a networking event hosted by her company. As she mingled with fellow professionals, she couldn't shake off the feeling of superficiality that permeated the room. People exchanged business cards and pleasantries, but there was little genuine connection or camaraderie.

Feeling disheartened, Sarah stepped outside for some fresh air. As she leaned against the railing, lost in her thoughts, she struck up a conversation with a stranger who had also stepped out for a breather. His name was Alex, and he was a freelance graphic designer attending the event.

Unlike the forced interactions inside, Sarah found herself engaged in a genuine conversation with Alex. They talked about their passions, their struggles, and their aspirations. There was an instant connection—a sense of authenticity that had been missing from Sarah's interactions for so long.

As the evening progressed, Sarah and Alex continued to chat, exchanging stories and laughter. Eventually, they parted ways with a promise to stay in touch. Little did Sarah know, this encounter would mark the beginning of a profound and genuine friendship.

Over the following weeks, Sarah and Alex kept their promise, meeting up for coffee or lunch whenever their busy schedules allowed. They shared not only their successes but also their failures, supporting and encouraging each other every step of the way. Through their genuine relationship, Sarah discovered the immense value of building authentic connections.

Sarah's experience with Alex taught her several important lessons about building genuine relationships:

1. Be Authentic: Authenticity breeds authenticity. Sarah realized that by being herself and sharing her true thoughts and feelings, she was able to attract like-minded individuals like Alex into her life. Authenticity lays the foundation for meaningful connections built on trust and mutual respect.

2. Listen Actively: Genuine relationships are not just about talking; they're also about listening. Sarah learned the importance of being present and attentive when interacting with others. By actively listening to Alex's stories and experiences, she showed him that she valued and respected his perspective.

3. Show Empathy: Empathy is key to forging deep connections with others. Sarah discovered that by empathizing with Alex's struggles and celebrating his successes, she could strengthen their bond and foster a sense of belonging and understanding.

4. Invest Time and Effort: Building genuine relationships takes time and effort. Sarah realized that she had to be willing to invest in her connections, whether it meant making time for coffee dates or offering a listening ear during challenging times. The effort she put into nurturing her friendship with Alex paid off in the form of a meaningful and fulfilling relationship.

5. Be Vulnerable: Vulnerability is a sign of strength, not weakness. Sarah understood that by being vulnerable and sharing her own insecurities and fears with Alex, she was able to deepen their connection and create a safe space for open and honest communication.

6. Celebrate Differences: Diversity enriches relationships. Sarah and Alex came from different backgrounds and had different perspectives, but instead of seeing these differences as barriers, they embraced them as opportunities for growth and learning.

Through her friendship with Alex, Sarah learned that genuine relationships are the cornerstone of a fulfilling life. They provide support, companionship, and a sense of belonging that cannot be found in superficial interactions. By approaching relationships with authenticity, empathy, and vulnerability, Sarah was able to cultivate a deep and lasting connection that enriched her life in ways she never imagined possible.

In the end, Sarah realized that true happiness lies not in the number of connections she had but in the depth and authenticity of those connections. And as she continued her journey through life, she carried with her the invaluable lesson that building genuine relationships is not only important but essential for a life well-lived.

AUTHENTIC COMMUNICATION

Authentic communication is the cornerstone of meaningful connections and relationships. It involves expressing oneself genuinely, honestly, and transparently, without pretense or manipulation. In contrast, fake or poor communication often stems from a lack of sincerity, misunderstanding, or hidden agendas. Let's explore some real-life examples to illustrate the difference between fake/poor communication and authentic communication.

EXAMPLE 1: WORKPLACE SCENARIO

Fake/Poor Communication:

In a corporate setting, imagine a manager who gives vague, insincere feedback to their employees during performance reviews. Instead of providing constructive criticism and actionable feedback, they offer generic compliments or sugar-coated criticisms to avoid confrontation or discomfort. For instance, they might say, "You're doing fine, but there's always room for improvement," without offering specific areas for growth or development. This type of communication leaves employees feeling confused, undervalued, and unsure about how to improve.

Authentic Communication:

In contrast, an authentic manager engages in open, honest, and constructive communication with their team members. They provide specific, actionable feedback that acknowledges both strengths and areas for improvement. For example, they might say, "I appreciate your dedication and creativity in handling project X. However, I noticed that there were some missed deadlines. Let's discuss strategies to improve time management and prioritize tasks effectively." This type of communication fosters trust, growth, and mutual respect within the team.

EXAMPLE 2: PERSONAL RELATIONSHIPS

Fake/Poor Communication:

Consider a romantic relationship where one partner consistently avoids addressing issues or expressing their true feelings out of fear of conflict or rejection. Instead of openly communicating their concerns or desires, they resort to passive-aggressive behavior or silent treatment. For instance, they might give the silent treatment after an argument instead of engaging in a constructive dialogue to resolve conflicts. This type of communication leads to misunderstandings, resentment, and emotional distance between partners.

Authentic Communication:

In contrast, authentic communication in relationships involves vulnerability, empathy, and active listening. For example, a partner might express their feelings openly and honestly, even if it involves discomfort or vulnerability. They communicate their needs, boundaries, and concerns respectfully, without resorting to passive-aggressive tactics. For instance, they might say, "I felt hurt when you canceled our plans without discussing it with me first. Can we talk about how we can prioritize our time together?" This type of communication fosters intimacy, trust, and mutual understanding in relationships.

EXAMPLE 3: SOCIAL INTERACTIONS

Fake/Poor Communication:

In social settings, imagine a person who engages in superficial small talk and pretends to be someone they're not to fit in or impress others. They might exaggerate their accomplishments, downplay their vulnerabilities, or agree with others' opinions even if they disagree. For example, they might nod along with a controversial statement to avoid confrontation or maintain a facade of agreeability. This type of communication lacks authenticity and genuine connection.

Authentic Communication:

Authentic communication in social interactions involves being true to oneself and engaging with others authentically. Instead of pretending to be someone they're not, an authentic individual expresses their thoughts, feelings, and opinions sincerely. They engage in meaningful conversations, listen actively, and share their authentic selves without fear of judgment. For example, they might respectfully express their disagreement with a controversial statement and engage in a constructive dialogue to explore different perspectives. This type of communication fosters genuine connections and deeper relationships.

In summary, authentic communication is characterized by sincerity, honesty, vulnerability, and mutual respect. It involves expressing oneself genuinely and engaging with others authentically, without pretense or manipulation. In contrast, fake or poor communication often stems from fear, insecurity, or hidden agendas, leading to misunderstandings, resentment, and disconnection. By practicing authentic communication in various aspects of life, we can cultivate deeper connections, foster trust, and build more fulfilling relationships.

TRUST AND INTIMACY

Trust and intimacy are foundational elements in any meaningful relationship, whether it's romantic, familial, or platonic. Cultivating trust and intimacy requires vulnerability, honesty, and empathy. Real-life examples can shed light on how to build and recognize these qualities.

To cultivate trust, honesty is paramount. Being truthful in both words and actions builds a solid foundation of trust. For example, imagine a friendship where one friend consistently cancels plans last minute with vague excuses. On the other hand, another friend communicates openly about their availability and commitments. Over time, the latter friend earns trust through their consistent honesty and reliability.

Consistency is another key quality in building trust. People need to feel confident that they can rely on someone's words and actions over time. Consider a business partnership where one partner consistently meets deadlines and delivers quality work, while the other partner frequently misses deadlines and offers excuses. The reliable partner earns trust through their consistent performance, while the unreliable partner undermines trust with their inconsistency.

Transparency is also crucial in cultivating trust. Open communication and a willingness to share thoughts, feelings, and intentions foster trust and intimacy. For instance, in a romantic relationship, one partner may have insecurities about their finances. By openly discussing their concerns and financial situation with their partner, they build trust and intimacy through vulnerability and transparency.

Another essential quality in building trust is integrity. Acting in alignment with one's values and principles, even when no one is watching, demonstrates integrity. For example, in a workplace setting, a manager who consistently upholds ethical standards and treats employees with fairness and respect earns trust through their integrity.

Empathy is a vital component of building trust and intimacy. Showing understanding and compassion towards others' experiences and emotions fosters deeper connections. Consider a situation where a friend is going through a difficult time. Offering a listening ear, validating their feelings, and providing support demonstrates empathy and strengthens trust and intimacy in the friendship.

When assessing whether to trust someone, several signs can indicate their trustworthiness. Consistency in words and actions is a significant indicator. Pay attention to whether someone follows through on their promises and commitments consistently over time. If someone's behavior is erratic or inconsistent, it may be a red flag for trustworthiness.

Another sign to look for is transparency. Is the person open and honest in their communication, or do they withhold information or dodge questions? Transparency builds trust by creating a sense of authenticity and reliability.

Integrity is also an important quality to observe. Consider whether the person acts in alignment with their stated values and principles, even in challenging situations. Someone who demonstrates integrity is more likely to be trustworthy.

Empathy is another key indicator of trustworthiness. Notice whether the person shows empathy and understanding towards others' emotions and experiences.

Empathetic individuals are more likely to prioritize honesty, fairness, and compassion in their interactions.

In real-life scenarios, trust and intimacy can be cultivated through shared experiences and mutual vulnerability. For example, in a romantic relationship, partners may gradually open up about their fears, insecurities, and past traumas, deepening their emotional connection and trust in each other.

In conclusion, trust and intimacy are essential ingredients in building meaningful relationships. Cultivating trust requires honesty, consistency, transparency, integrity, and empathy. By demonstrating these qualities in our interactions and paying attention to them in others, we can foster deeper connections and stronger bonds based on trust and intimacy.

PRACTICE

Practical Tasks:

1. Self-Reflection Exercise:

Take some time to reflect on your own values, interests, and aspirations. Consider what truly matters to you in your relationships and what qualities you value in others. Write down your thoughts and feelings in a journal or notebook. This exercise will help you gain clarity on your authentic self and what you seek in genuine relationships.

2. Authenticity Practice:

Engage in authentic communication with at least one person in your life each day. This could involve sharing your thoughts, feelings, or experiences openly and honestly, without fear of judgment or rejection. Practice active listening and empathy in your interactions, allowing others to express themselves authentically as well. Over time, this practice will strengthen your ability to build meaningful connections based on mutual trust and understanding.

3. Vulnerability Challenge:

Challenge yourself to embrace vulnerability in your relationships by sharing something personal or difficult with someone you trust. This could be a past mistake, a fear or insecurity, or a heartfelt confession. By allowing yourself to be vulnerable, you create space for deeper intimacy and connection with others. Pay attention to how this act of vulnerability strengthens your relationships and fosters a sense of authenticity and closeness.

CHAPTER SIX

LIVING AUTHENTICALLY

Living authentically is not about conforming to societal expectations or seeking approval from others. It's not about pretending to be someone you're not or suppressing your true thoughts, feelings, and desires to fit in. Authentic living rejects the notion of wearing masks to please others or maintain a facade of perfection. Instead, it's about embracing who you genuinely are, flaws and all, and aligning your actions with your inner values and beliefs.

Living authentically is not about seeking perfection. It's not about projecting an image of flawlessness or success at all costs. Authenticity acknowledges and embraces imperfection as an essential aspect of the human experience. It recognizes that making mistakes and experiencing failures are inevitable parts of growth and self-discovery. Rather than hiding these imperfections, authentic living encourages embracing them as opportunities for learning and personal development.

Living authentically is not about selfishness or disregarding the needs of others. It's not about pursuing personal interests or goals without considering the impact on those around you. Authenticity involves understanding and respecting both your own needs and the needs of others. It's about finding a balance between self-expression and empathy, recognizing that authenticity thrives in an environment of mutual respect and understanding.

Living authentically is not about stagnation or resisting change. It's not about clinging to outdated beliefs or habits simply because they feel familiar or comfortable. Authentic living involves embracing growth and evolution, being open to new experiences and perspectives, and adapting to life's inevitable transitions. It requires courage to confront uncertainty and step into the unknown, trusting in your ability to navigate whatever challenges may arise.

Living authentically is not about isolation or alienation from society. It's not about withdrawing from social interactions or relationships out of fear of judgment or rejection. Authenticity thrives in connection and community, fostering genuine connections based on mutual acceptance and understanding. It involves sharing your true self with others and creating meaningful connections built on trust, vulnerability, and honesty.

Living authentically is not about ignoring the realities of the world or avoiding responsibility. It's not about escaping from difficult situations or shirking accountability for your actions. Authentic living requires facing challenges head-on, taking ownership of your choices, and actively working towards positive change. It involves living with integrity and aligning your actions with your values, even when it's difficult or inconvenient.

Now, why is living authentically essential to true living and a life of fulfillment?

Living authentically is essential because it cultivates a deep sense of self-awareness and inner peace. When you embrace your true self and live in alignment with your values, you experience a profound sense of authenticity and integrity. This self-awareness allows you to make choices that are genuinely fulfilling and meaningful to you, rather than being driven by external expectations or societal pressures.

Living authentically fosters genuine connections and relationships. When you show up as your authentic self, you attract like-minded individuals who appreciate you for who you are. Authentic relationships are built on trust, respect, and mutual understanding, creating a supportive network of friends, family, and peers who uplift and empower each other.

Living authentically promotes personal growth and development. When you embrace authenticity, you open yourself up to new experiences, perspectives, and opportunities for learning. You become more resilient in the face of challenges and setbacks, knowing that you have the strength and courage to overcome obstacles and pursue your dreams.

Living authentically leads to greater satisfaction and fulfillment in life. When you live in alignment with your values and passions, you feel a sense of purpose and meaning that transcends material success or external validation. Authentic living allows you to tap into your unique talents and strengths, contributing to the world in a way that is deeply meaningful to you.

In point of fact, living authentically is not about conforming to societal norms or seeking perfection; it's about embracing your true self and living in alignment with your values and beliefs. Authentic living promotes self-awareness, genuine connections, personal growth, and fulfillment, ultimately leading to a more meaningful and satisfying life. By embracing authenticity, you can cultivate a sense of purpose and integrity that enriches every aspect of your existence.

ALIGNING ACTIONS WITH VALUES

Aligning actions with values is essential for anyone seeking success and fulfillment in their endeavors. Whether you're a crypto enthusiast, copywriter, affiliate marketer, banker, investor, or entrepreneur, integrating your values into your actions can lead to a more meaningful and satisfying journey. Let's explore practical steps for aligning actions with values, accompanied by real-life examples from individuals in various fields.

1. Identify Core Values: Begin by identifying your core values. These are the principles that guide your decisions and behaviors. They could include integrity, authenticity, innovation, compassion, or any other values that resonate with you. Take the time to reflect on what truly matters to you and prioritize these values in your life.

Example: Sarah, a copywriter, identifies integrity and creativity as her core values. She believes in delivering high-quality work that authentically represents her clients' brands while staying true to her creative vision.

2.Set Clear Goals: Once you've identified your values, set clear goals that align with them. Define what success means to you in terms of both professional achievements and personal fulfillment. Having clear goals helps you focus your actions and make decisions that are in line with your values.

Example: John, a crypto enthusiast, sets a goal to invest in projects that align with his values of sustainability and technological innovation. He researches and selects cryptocurrencies and blockchain projects that have a positive impact on the environment and society.

3.Integrate Values into Daily Practices: Incorporate your values into your daily practices and routines. This could involve setting intentions at the beginning of each day, reflecting on how your actions align with your values, and making adjustments as needed. Consistently practicing behaviors that reflect your values reinforces their importance in your life.

Example: Maria, an affiliate marketer, integrates her values of transparency and honesty into her marketing strategies. She discloses any affiliations and potential biases to her audience, building trust and credibility with her followers.

4. Seek Alignment in Career Choices: Choose career paths and opportunities that align with your values. Consider how your work contributes to the greater good and whether it reflects your core principles. If necessary, be willing to make changes or pivot towards roles that better align with your values.

Example: Michael, a banker, transitions to a role in impact investing after realizing that traditional banking practices conflict with his values of social responsibility and ethical finance. He channels his expertise into supporting projects that generate positive social and environmental outcomes alongside financial returns.

5. Practice Ethical Decision-Making: When faced with decisions, consider the ethical implications and how they align with your values. Take the time to evaluate potential outcomes and choose courses of action that uphold your principles, even if they may be more challenging or less lucrative in the short term.

Example: David, an investor, prioritizes ethical considerations when evaluating investment opportunities.

He conducts thorough due diligence to ensure that his investments support companies with strong ethical practices and sustainable business models, even if it means foregoing some potentially profitable opportunities.

6. **Lead by Example**: Whether you're an entrepreneur or a team member, lead by example and inspire others to align their actions with their values. Foster a culture of integrity, authenticity, and purpose within your workplace or community, encouraging others to do the same.

Example: Rachel, an entrepreneur, builds her company with a strong emphasis on social responsibility and environmental sustainability. She creates a values-driven organizational culture where employees are empowered to make decisions aligned with the company's mission and values.

No doubt, aligning actions with values is a transformative journey that requires self-awareness, intentionality, and commitment. By identifying core values, setting clear goals, integrating values into daily practices, seeking alignment in career choices, practicing ethical decision-making, and leading by example, individuals in any field can create a meaningful and fulfilling path to success. The real-life examples provided demonstrate how individuals from diverse backgrounds have successfully aligned their actions with their values, contributing to both personal fulfillment and positive impact in their respective industries.

EMBRACING IMPERFECTION

The profound wisdom encapsulated in the proverb, "The perfect is the enemy of the good," serves as a powerful reminder to embrace imperfection. This age-old saying, attributed to Voltaire, cuts through the illusion of perfection, urging us to recognize the beauty that lies within the imperfect and the incomplete.

At its core, this proverb challenges the paralyzing pursuit of flawlessness, encouraging us to acknowledge that waiting for perfection can hinder progress and rob us of the richness inherent in the imperfect. Let us delve into the heart of this proverb, exploring how its timeless wisdom can be a catalyst for change, pushing us to embrace imperfection and embark on a journey of self-discovery and growth.

The quest for perfection is a pervasive force in modern society, fueled by societal expectations, the pursuit of success, and the pervasive influence of social media. We are bombarded with images of seemingly flawless lives, airbrushed bodies, and meticulously curated lifestyles. In this pursuit of an unattainable perfection, we often overlook the beauty that resides within the imperfect, the authentic, and the real.

"The perfect is the enemy of the good" speaks directly to this phenomenon, warning us against the pitfalls of perfectionism. It invites us to reevaluate our standards and question whether the relentless pursuit of perfection is hindering our ability to appreciate the beauty that exists in the here and now. Instead of waiting for the perfect moment, the perfect idea, or the perfect self, the proverb urges us to embrace the good – the imperfect, the incomplete, and the genuine.

Imperfection is not a sign of failure but rather a testament to our humanity. In the pursuit of perfection, we often overlook the valuable lessons and experiences that come with embracing imperfection. Think about a time when you hesitated to start a project or take a leap because conditions weren't ideal or the plan wasn't flawless. The proverb serves as a wake-up call, reminding us that waiting for perfection can lead to missed opportunities and unrealized potential.

Moreover, the proverb encourages us to view imperfection as a catalyst for growth. In the face of imperfection, we are challenged to adapt, innovate, and find creative solutions. The imperfections in our work, relationships, and personal endeavors are not roadblocks but rather stepping stones towards improvement and progress. They are opportunities to learn, iterate, and refine ourselves.

THE JOURNEY TO AUTHENTICITY

The journey to authenticity stands as a beacon of hope, guiding individuals towards a life of genuine self-expression and fulfillment. It is a journey marked by courage, self-discovery, and transformation, offering the promise of liberation from the chains of fear and insecurity.

At its core, authenticity is about being true to oneself – embracing one's values, passions, and unique identity without reservation or apology. Yet, for many, the path to authenticity can seem daunting, fraught with uncertainty and the fear of judgment. It's easy to feel overwhelmed by the pressures of societal expectations, to doubt oneself in the face of perceived inadequacies, or to fear rejection for daring to be different.

But here's the truth: Authenticity is not reserved for the select few; it is a birthright inherent in every individual. It is a journey that anyone can embark upon, regardless of their background, circumstances, or past experiences. And it is a journey that is not only worthwhile but also entirely within reach.

The first step on this journey is self-awareness – the willingness to look inward and confront the truths that lie beneath the surface. It involves asking oneself tough questions, exploring one's values, passions, strengths, and weaknesses, and coming to terms with the complexities of one's identity. Self-awareness is the foundation upon which authenticity is built, providing the clarity and insight necessary to navigate the challenges ahead.

Once armed with self-awareness, the next step is to challenge limiting beliefs – those deeply ingrained notions that tell us we must conform to certain standards or meet others' expectations to be accepted or successful. It's about recognizing that authenticity is not a liability but a strength, and that true fulfillment comes from embracing one's uniqueness rather than striving to fit into predefined molds.

With limiting beliefs cast aside, the journey to authenticity becomes a series of small but meaningful steps. It's about setting boundaries and asserting oneself, speaking up for what matters, pursuing passions and interests that ignite the soul, and surrounding oneself with people who uplift and support one's authentic self-expression. It's about being willing to take risks, make mistakes, and learn and grow from each experience along the way.

Yet, perhaps the most powerful aspect of the journey to authenticity is the sense of liberation it brings. As one sheds the layers of pretense and embraces their true self, they find a newfound sense of freedom – freedom from the need for external validation, freedom from the shackles of fear and insecurity, and freedom to live a life that is truly their own.

It's important to remember that the journey to authenticity is not without its challenges. There will be moments of doubt, moments of fear, and moments of vulnerability. But with each challenge comes an opportunity – an opportunity to reaffirm one's commitment to authenticity, to cultivate resilience in the face of adversity, and to emerge stronger and more empowered than ever before.

So, to anyone embarking on the journey to authenticity, know this: You are capable. You are worthy. And you are not alone. Embrace the journey with an open heart and a courageous spirit, and trust that the path will unfold before you as you walk it. And remember, the world doesn't need more imitations; it needs more originals – more individuals who dare to be themselves, fully and unapologetically.

PRACTICE

1. Values Clarification Exercise: Begin by identifying your core values. Take some time to reflect on what truly matters to you in life. Write down a list of values that resonate with you, such as honesty, compassion, creativity, or freedom. Then, prioritize these values based on their importance to you. This exercise will help you gain clarity on what drives you and what you want to prioritize in your life, guiding you towards living authentically in alignment with your values.

2. Authenticity Journal: Start an authenticity journal to track your thoughts, feelings, and experiences related to living authentically. Each day, take a few minutes to reflect on moments when you felt true to yourself and moments when you may have veered off course. Consider what factors contributed to these experiences and how you can cultivate more authenticity in your daily life. Use your journal as a tool for self-reflection and growth, noting any patterns or insights that emerge along the way.

3. Courageous Action Plan: Develop a plan for taking courageous actions aligned with your authentic self. Start by identifying one area of your life where you feel compelled to be more authentic but may be holding back due to fear or insecurity. Break down this larger goal into smaller, manageable steps, each representing a courageous action you can take. Set specific deadlines and accountability measures to ensure you follow through. By taking deliberate steps towards authenticity, you'll gradually build confidence and momentum in living authentically.

....

Special note to the reader:

Prince William
Wishes you success on the Journey of Authenticity!

9 798883 160737